IRISH
BABY NAMES

Féilim O'Connor has a lifetime of first-hand experience with what it's like to have an Irish name people struggle to pronounce. Up until his teenage years, he was the recipient of many a birthday card addressed to Faylum, Pheidhelm and Philim.

Morgan Buckley is an Irish songwriter, music producer and record label manager. Apart from writing books, Morgan can be found 'ghostwriting' songs for big acts in London.

Gavin Drea is an Irish actor, writer and comedian. He can be seen on Apple, Netflix, Amazon and Disney. He's a founding member of the comedy collective Dreamgun.

Féilim, Morgan and Gavin have been friends since getting caught talking together at the back of Irish class.

IRISH BABY NAMES

WHAT THEY MEAN *and*
HOW *to* **PRONOUNCE THEM**

FÉILIM O'CONNOR,
MORGAN BUCKLEY and GAVIN DREA

GILL BOOKS

Gill Books
Hume Avenue
Park West
Dublin 12
www.gillbooks.ie

Gill Books is an imprint of M.H. Gill and Co.

© Féilim O'Connor, Morgan Buckley and Gavin Drea 2025

978 18045 82497

Designed by Sara Miranda
Illustrated by Conor Nolan
Edited by Esther Ní Dhonnacha
Proofread by Gráinne Treanor
Printed and bound by Scandbook, Sweden
This book is typeset in Futura and Pasta & Wine

The paper used in this book comes from the wood pulp of sustainably managed forests.

All rights reserved.

No part of this publication may be copied, reproduced or transmitted in any form or by any means, without written permission of the publishers. To the best of our knowledge, this book complies in full with the requirements of the General Product Safety Regulation (GPSR). For further information and help with any safety queries, please contact us at productsafety@gill.ie

A CIP catalogue record for this book is available from the British Library.

5 4 3 2 1

To the three queens who bore the babies who wrote this book: Elizabeth, Jeanne and Marion.

And to the three goddesses who supported us during its creation: Géraldine, Tara and Roisin.

CONTENTS

08 Introduction

19 Mispronounced Names We Love to Hear

33 Irish From Afar but Far from Irish

44 Wild Child Names

60 Lost Treasures

79 Names from Irish Mythology

94 Names by Geography

107 Popular Irish Names Today

136 Stories Behind Irish Surnames

141 Names by Numbers

INTRODUCTION

Irish names: they're older than the Pyramids, and looking to the future, they'll probably be mispronounced for another 5,000 years. This book is a way to navigate Irish names, travelling through their mystical and mysterious soundscapes, so that you can endow your baby with the perfect name. Ireland is a land of poets and jokers, lovers and warriors, drinkers and thinkers. It might seem like the classic Irish names are Mary and Joseph, but in fact they're about as Irish as the Pope. We're bringing you back, way back, before Christianity came to these shores, to rediscover Irish names from an ancient Ireland of mystery, magic and mythos. An Irish name is probably the greatest first gift you can give a child, whatever their future holds.

There are quite a few girls' names in Irish that translate to 'beauty'. And a lot of boys' names are linked to bravery. Safe to say there was a lot of fighting back then. But the meaning of a name is often just the first layer. Digging a little deeper, you'll find references to the landscape, wild animals and ancient Irish sovereignty.

The names in this book are broken into various categories, including mispronounced names, mythology, geography, and wild child names. So no matter the type of name you're looking for, you'll find it here. Explanations are short and to the point because, well, let's be honest, our attention spans are finite these days. And with a baby on the way, no doubt you have your hands full.

You'll get the meaning for each name, as well as variations, so you can decide on your preferred spelling. You'll see a guide for the most common pronunciation, but bear in mind that pronunciation often varies by dialect. You may be more familiar with a Fionn who pronounces it 'finn' or an Áine who pronounces it 'en-ya'. For every name, you also have some data on the popularity of the name – the number of births in Ireland in the most recent record, as well as its popularity way back in 1964 (when the government first started keeping count of baby names for each year). Note that if a name was used three times or fewer in a given year, it doesn't make the official list and is recorded as 'no record'.

While this book is a comprehensive list of Irish names, it's not exhaustive. Exhaustive is exhausting and that's for another book. We've tried to select names from the almost limitless number of Irish words that could be used for a name. Irish is a very old language with a great variety of words. For example, there are thirty-two Irish words for 'field'. (One of them, cathairín, is a field containing a fairy dwelling. From this you can find similar sounding boys' names likes Cathair and Cathal.)

Throughout the great annals of Irish antiquity, there are countless heroes who have kept these names alive. If you choose one of these names for your son or daughter, they too might go on to become an Irish legend.

The names in this collection come from three main sources: 2024 record data, the oldest available Irish records (1964), and ancient Irish folklore. We've aimed to balance popular Irish names that are still widely used today with some ancient names from Irish mythology that we feel have been overlooked and are deserving of a revival.

Irish Names For Beginners

It might seem daunting for someone with only a smattering of Irish to start looking into Irish names. They can be hard to pronounce and there are endless names to get through. While pronunciation can be a little tricky, spelling often borders on utter madness. We're looking at you, Conchobhar! (pronounced Kru-hoor).

In Ireland, there might be about thirty or so names each year that are really popular, but after that they taper off very quickly. Many of them you might have already heard of. One of the big aims of this book is to give you a balanced view of some of the better-known timeless classic Irish names, while also giving you a glimpse into some real rarities with great acoustic qualities and historic value.

It may surprise you to learn that nowadays in Ireland there are more girls being given the names Poppy and Hope than Bridget and Fiona. With this book we hope to reignite an interest in some of the pre-Christian Irish names.

Let's get pagan, baby.

The Old Irish Alphabet

The English alphabet has 26 letters. Irish is a little different. The ancient Gaelic language had 16 letters. Modern Irish added two letters, H and P. This has resulted in the following 18-letter alphabet.

A B C D E F G H I L M N O P R S T U

So if you meet a man in the pub with the name 'Jkqvwxyz', claiming he's two-thirds Irish, one of you is probably drunk.

The Ogham Alphabet

The Ogham alphabet is a unique alphabet in both form and structure, consisting of a series of lines or notches inscribed vertically on the edge of a stone pillar, making it distinctive from most Western alphabets, which are written horizontally. Each letter takes its name from a plant species (around 360 of these have been found in Ireland).

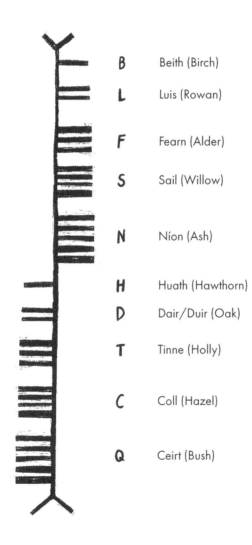

B — Beith (Birch)
L — Luis (Rowan)
F — Fearn (Alder)
S — Sail (Willow)
N — Níon (Ash)
H — Huath (Hawthorn)
D — Dair/Duir (Oak)
T — Tinne (Holly)
C — Coll (Hazel)
Q — Ceirt (Bush)

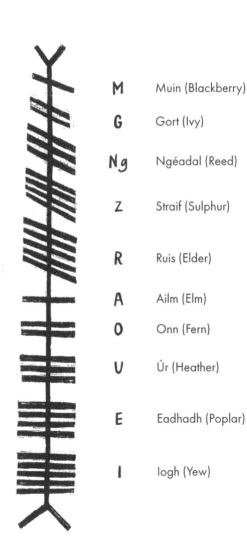

M	Muin (Blackberry)
G	Gort (Ivy)
Ng	Ngéadal (Reed)
Z	Straif (Sulphur)
R	Ruis (Elder)
A	Ailm (Elm)
O	Onn (Fern)
U	Úr (Heather)
E	Eadhadh (Poplar)
I	Iogh (Yew)

Mythology Family Tree

Ireland is old. Very old. For centuries, its myths and legends were passed down through oral traditions of bards and storytellers: wild tales of druids, cyclopes, godlike warriors and shapeshifters. Here is the family tree to help you make sense of this almost forgotten weird old world. Perhaps it's time for a family reunion.

The Dagda

The chief god of the Tuatha Dé Danann or 'tribe of the gods', a supernatural race in Irish mythology.

Dian Cecht

Dian Cecht is the god of healing in Irish mythology, and the healer of the Tuatha Dé Danann.

Balor

The cyclopean leader of the Fomorians, a band of malicious supernatural creatures.

Cian (Scal Balb)

A son of the Tuatha Dé Danann.

Ethnia

Daughter of Balor.

Lugh
Son of a Tuatha Dé Danann and a Fomorian princess, Lugh bridges the gap between light and darkness.

Deichtine
Cú Chulainn's mother, a warrior and charioteer.

Aife
A skilled warrior and rival to Scáthach. She fell in love with Cú Chulainn and bore him a son, Connla.

Cú Chulainn (Setanta)
The Hound of Culann, Cú Chulainn is one of the most iconic heroes in Irish folklore.

Connla
Also known as Conlaoch, he was Cú Chulainn's only son and was ultimately accidently killed by his own father in a case of mistaken identity.

The Gaelic Tree Alphabet

Trees undeniably held deep spiritual importance for the Celts, who believed different species embodied unique energies and revered certain ones, like oak, hazel and yew, as especially sacred. They might provide you with inspiration for an unusual baby name.

A *Ailm* (Elm Tree)

B *Beith* (Birch Tree)

C *Coll* (Hazel Tree)

D *Dair/Duir* (Oak Tree)

E *Eadhadh* (Poplar Tree)

G *Gort* (Ivy)

F *Fearn* (Alder Tree)

H *Huath* (Hawthorn Tree)

I *Iogh* (Yew Tree)

L *Luis* (Rowan Tree)

M *Muin* (Blackberry)

N *Níon* (Ash Tree)

O *Onn* (Fern)

P *Peith Bhog* (Downy Birch)

R *Ruis* (Elder Tree)

S *Sail* (Willow Tree)

T *Teine* (Holly)

U *Úr* (Heather)

Wait, one last thing ... what's up with the fada?

Ah yes, the form-filling nightmare that is the fada. If you are fortunate enough not to know what this is, the fada is a little slanted dash that goes over a vowel in the Irish language. It tells you that the vowel is to be pronounced long. It can be found everywhere in Ireland, even in the word for Ireland itself, Éire.

Despite being a vital ingredient for many Irish names, fadas were not officially recorded in the Irish 1964 census, which is when modern records first began. You can thank those English typewriters for that. While you might be tempted to leave out this keyboard challenge, be brave and add a dash of flavour to an Irish name. We simply love them and would encourage you to keep them.

MISPRONOUNCED
NAMES we LOVE to HEAR

So you want to have your name spelt correctly on a Starbucks cup?

Well, let us introduce you to ...

GIRLS' NAMES

Méabh

Pronunciation: Mayv
Variations: Maeve, Méibh, Medb, Meadhbh

This name means 'intoxicating'. Medb was the warrior queen of Connacht in Irish mythology. She was a fearless and cunning heroine and according to a collection of early Irish texts – the *Dindshenchas* – was known as the fair-haired wolf queen.

Latest record: Méabh ranked 50 with 104 newborns.
When records began: Maeve ranked 80 with 74 newborns.

Aoibhe

Pronunciation: Ave-a
Variations: Aoibhinn, Aoibheann, Aoibhínn, Aoibheann

In Irish *aoibh* means 'beauty', which unsurprisingly is a word that has lent itself to a number of old Irish names. In Irish mythology, the main character is usually introduced as the best looking; a great name for the soon-to-be main character in your story.

Latest record: Aoibhe ranked 156 with 29 newborns.
When records began: No record.

Saoirse

Pronunciation: Seer-shuh

Saoirse is a name that's rising in popularity recently in Ireland. Its recent rise is due in part to the rising star herself, Saoirse Ronan. This name definitely gets an Oscar nomination from us. The Irish word *saoirse* has a lovely meaning behind it, standing for both liberty and craftsmanship.

Latest record: Saoirse ranked 24 with 164 newborns.
When records began: No record.

Niamh

Pronunciation: It's not Neome, it's NEEEV!

In the Irish language, the word *niamh* means 'brightness and lustre'. The name also belongs to an important character in Irish mythology: Niamh lived in the land of eternal youth, called Tír na nÓg.

Latest record: Niamh ranked 94 with 51 newborns.
When records began: Niamh ranked 109 with 53 newborns.

Siobhán

Pronunciation: Sh-vawn
Variations: Siobhan, Shevaun, Shivaun

Siobhán is a wonderfully Irish-sounding name that means 'God is gracious'. Its origin is not Irish but comes from the Hebrew, a name which we would know as Ioanna.

Latest record: No record.
When records began: Siobhan ranked 35 with 207 newborns.

Aífe

Pronunciation: Ee-fa
Variation: Aoife

There are two spellings of this name, the somewhat popular Aoife, with an 'o', and the much lesser-known Aífe, with an 'i'. We are fond of the version with the 'i', just like the Irish goddess Aífe, who battled head on against one of greatest Irish warriors, Cú Chulainn. In the end, it was love, not war, between the two and they had a son together, Connla.

Latest record: Aoife ranked 45 with 107 newborns.
When records began: Aoife ranked 206 with 13 newborns.

Róisín

Pronunciation: Roe-sheen
Variations: Roisin, Roisín, Roísin, Róise

Coming from the Irish word for 'rose', *rós*. The '-ín' implies 'small'. So this beautiful name means 'little rose'. Thin Lizzy had a song and full album called *Róisín Dubh*, meaning 'Black Rose' – an album about Irish legends from long ago.

In Irish mythology, the Róisín Dubh was the symbol on the robes of the Druids of Ireland, an ancient high-ranking class who were considered godlike because of their knowledge of nature.

Latest record: Róisín ranked 33 with 126 newborns.
When records began: Roisin ranked 154 with 24 newborns.

Caoimhe

Pronunciation: Kwee-va

Caoimhe – surely there's a letter 'v' in there somewhere? Nope. It's 'mh' in Irish that gives that sound. Caoimhe comes from the Irish word *caomh*, meaning 'companion' or 'gentle friend'.

Latest record: Caoimhe ranked 31 with 131 newborns.
When records began: No record.

Gráinne

Pronunciation: Grawn-yeh
Variation: Grace

Gráinne has ties to the Irish words *grian* (sun), *gráinne* (grain) and *grá* (love). Grace O'Malley was a fearsome pirate queen who led twenty ships and over 200 men.

Latest record: Gráinne ranked 259 with 16 newborns.
When records began: Grainne ranked 62 with 99 newborns.

Sinéad

Pronunciation: Shin-ade

Another name to mean 'God is gracious'. While there aren't many ancient Irish legends with this name, there's certainly a modern one: Sinéad O'Connor. Nothing compares to this name.

Latest record: Sinéad ranked 342 with 11 newborns.
When records began: Sinead ranked 109 with 53 newborns.

Asthore

Pronunciation: As-tore

From the Irish word *stór*, this name translates as 'my treasure'. With no records of this name, it's a rare treasure indeed. It's a lovely name for a girl or a boy. *A stór mo chroí*: treasure of my heart.

No record.

BOYS' NAMES

Tadhg

Pronunciation: Tige (like 'tiger' without the 'r')
Variations: Tadgh

Despite this name looking like it was invented by someone who's losing a game of Scrabble, it actually means 'poet' or 'storyteller' and should be handed down to future wordsmiths.

Latest record: Tadhg ranked 6 with 318 newborns.
When records began: Tadg ranked 232 with 3 newborns.

Eóghan

Pronunciation: Owe-en
Variations: Eoghan, Eóin, Eoin

Coming from the old Irish words *eó*, meaning 'yew tree', and *ghan*, meaning 'born of'. This spelling is closer to the old Irish Eógan, whereas in modern Irish it's much more common to see the name spelled without the fada.

Latest record: No record.
When records began: Eoghan ranked 164 with 9 newborns.

Niall

Pronunciation: Knee-al
Variation: Neil

Our very own Genghis Khan. The Uí Néill dynasty (literally translated as 'descendants of Niall') is said to have three million descendants today.

Latest record: Niall ranked 174 with 29 newborns.
When records began: Niall ranked 47 with 142 newborns.

Ciarán

Pronunciation: Keer-awn
Variations: Ciaran, Kieran

Ciarán means 'little dark one'. The popularity of this name has dropped off a cliff in recent years. We hope it has brighter years ahead, as it's a strong and warm Irish name.

Latest record: Ciarán ranked 200 with 24 newborns.
When records began: Ciaran ranked 49 with 124 newborns.

Cian

Pronunciation: Key-un
Variation: Cianán

Cian means 'ancient' or 'resilient'. In Ireland, everyone knows a Cian. This name, although very Irish, also works internationally, as it is easy to pronounce.

Latest record: Cian ranked 33 with 158 newborns.
When records began: No record.

Donnacha

Pronunciation: Done-ah-kha
Variations: Donnchadh, Donncha

Donnacha means 'brown-haired warrior' and was the name of a famous Irish High King.

Latest record: Donnacha ranked 65 with 88 newborns.
When records began: No record.

Féilim

Pronunciation: Fay-lum
Variations: Feidhelm, Féidhlim, Phelim

Féilim means 'beauty' and 'ever-good'. It's also the name of one of the authors of this book, so we couldn't agree more with this definition.

Latest record: Féilim ranked 275 with 15 newborns.
When records began: Phelim ranked 170 with 9 newborns.

Ruairí

Pronunciation: Roor-ee
Variations: Ruaidhrí, Rory

Ruairí means 'the fiery-haired king'. In Irish mythology Ruairí was the last High King of Ireland before the Anglo-Normans invaded.

Latest record: Ruairí ranked 98 with 57 newborns.
When records began: Rory ranked 73 with 56 newborns.

Odhrán

Pronunciation: Oh-rawn – the 'd' is a silent delight.
Variation: Odhran

This name is said to come from the old Irish word *odhar*, which can mean anything from pale, to dark, to green in the middle. Not a bad attempt at describing the colour palette of the Irish landscape.

Latest record: Odhrán ranked 81 with 73 newborns.
When records began: No record.

Pádraig

Pronunciation: Paw-drig
Variation: Patrick

Pádraig is the Irish for Patrick. In more recent Irish history, Saint Patrick is our primary patron saint. Did he drive out snakes from Ireland? Almost certainly not, as there's never been so much as a fossil of a snake found here. But will we continue to celebrate and drink like he did? Of course we will.

Latest record: Pádraig ranked 214 with 22 newborns.
When records began: Padraig ranked 88 with 38 newborns.

IRISH FROM AFAR
BUT FAR *from* IRISH

*These non-traditional Irish names
have taken on lives of their own abroad.*

GIRLS' NAMES

Shannon

Pronunciation: Shan-un

A common name in America but actually much less common in Ireland. The word may have come from *sion*, meaning 'wise', and *abhainn*, meaning 'river', and has also been translated as 'calm water'. Ireland's largest river is called the Shannon, *An tSionainn*.

No record.

Erin

Pronunciation: Air-in
Variations: Éire, Éirinn, Éireann, Eira

This comes from the Irish word for Ireland, which is spelt *Éire*.

Latest record: Erin ranked 35 with 120 newborns.
When records began: No record.

Riley

Pronunciation: Rye-lee

While this name could come from the Old English meaning 'rye clearing', it may also have roots in the family name Ó Raghallaigh, anglicised as O'Reilly.

Latest record: Riley ranked 197 with 22 newborns.
When records began: No record.

Nevaeh

Pronunciation: Nah-vay-ah

Believed by some to be a variation on the Irish name Niamh, this name is actually an English word spelt backwards: 'heaven'.

Latest record: Nevaeh ranked 223 with 19 newborns.
When records began: No record.

Colleen

Pronunciation: Koh-leen

Part of the reason this isn't popular in Ireland is that it's a direct anglicisation of the word for 'girl', *cailín*. It's taken on huge popularity among second- and third-generation Irish emigrants, from America to Australia.

No record.

Sloane

Pronunciation: Slown (rhymes with 'flown')

Possibly linked to the Irish word *slua* meaning 'host', 'force' or 'army', this could be a good name for a scrappy young one.

Latest record: Sloane ranked 342 with 11 newborns.
When records began: No record.

Kayleigh

Pronunciation: Kay-lee
Variations: Caoilinn, Caoileann, Caoilfhionn

This one is a bit of an Americanism, as there's no 'k' in the Irish alphabet. That being said, the Irish for slender is *caol*, which is where the name Kayleigh comes from.

Latest record: Kayleigh ranked 171 with 26 newborns.
When records began: No record.

Sibéal

Pronunciation: Shih-bail

The name came in with the Normans in the form of Isabelle. *Sibéal* broadly means 'oath-keeper'. In ancient Greece, the Sibyls were oracles who had the ability to tell the future and were connected to the spiritual world. This name is on the rise in recent years.

Latest record: Sibéal ranked 342 with 11 newborns.
When records began: No record.

Shauna

Pronunciation: Shaw-nah
Variation: Seána

The luscious Irish name Shauna actually originates from the ancient Hebrew name Yohanan.

Latest record: Shauna ranked 631 with 5 newborns.
When records began: No record.

BOYS' NAMES

Quinn

Pronunciation: Kwin

A hugely popular first name in America, Quinn is a well-known surname in Ireland. From old Irish *ceann*, meaning 'head' or 'chieftain'.

Latest record: Quinn ranked 394 with 9 newborns.
When records began: No record.

Eamon

Pronunciation: Aim-un
Variations: Éamon, Éamonn, Eadhmonn

Eamon is actually the Irish version of the Old English name Edmund or Edward. From the old English words *ead*, meaning 'wealth', and *mund*, meaning 'guardian', this name means 'rich protector'. Although until the baby gets a job ... you might have to be theirs.

Latest record: Eamon ranked 350 with 11 newborns
When records began: Eamon ranked 62 with 86 newborns.

Maitiú

Pronunciation: Mat-chew
Variations: Maiú, Maidiú

Maitiú is derived from Matthew, one of the Twelve Apostles.

Latest record: Maitiú ranked 472 with 7 newborns
When records began: Matthew ranked 59 with 89 newborns.

Peadar

Pronunciation: Pad-der

While the name Peadar just feels wholly Irish – sounding like a third stage of evolution from Patrick to Pádraig to Peadar – it actually comes from the Latin for rock, 'petrus'. So for us, the name Peadar sounds like a rock-solid choice.

Latest record: Peadar ranked 231 with 19 newborns.
When records began: No record.

Gearóid

Pronunciation: Gar-owed
Variation: Gearoid

Gearóid is another name that came into Ireland during the Norman invasions. It is unsurprising that the Irish took a shine to this name, made up of the words for 'spear' and 'brave'. Cú Chulainn's famous spear, the Gáe Bulg, is Ireland's definitive weapon from early mythology and this name embodies its spirit fittingly.

Latest record: Gearóid ranked 252 with 17 newborns.
When records began: Gearoid ranked 164 with 9 newborns.

Seosamh

Pronunciation: Show-suv
Variation: Joseph

Look up Seosamh in an Irish dictionary and it'll simply tell you it's the Irish version of Joseph – yes, as in the father of baby Jesus himself. Naturally, Mary and Joseph were all the rage back when saint names were in fashion in the '60s. But since then, Joseph's been slipping down the charts. And Seosamh? Well, he never really had a moment in the spotlight to begin with.

Latest record: No record.
When records began: Seosamh ranked 214 with 4 newborns.

Amhlaoibh

Pronunciation: Ow-leev
Variation: Olaf

Amhlaoibh is the Irish version of the name Olaf. In the late 2000s to early 2010s Olaf popped up a handful of times in the records, but the name is certainly a rarity. Olaf is a strong, masculine Norse name that came in with the Vikings, and several Norwegian kings bore this name.

No record.

Pól

Pronunciation: Pole

Usually it's the Irish names that are being anglicised. In this case, the name Paul is being gaelicised. We shtuck a fada on it and called it our own. Paul actually comes from the Latin word *Paulus*, which means 'small' or 'humble'.

No record.

Bono

Pronunciation: Bon-oh

Bono – no, it's not Irish. It's actually Latin for 'I rock'; *bono, bonus, bonum*. Only messing. He may not be in the top of the charts anymore but he's made this list.

Latest record and when records began: Just the one (thankfully).

WILD
CHILD NAMES

*Ireland used to be a pretty wild place.
Wolves inhabited the Emerald Isle up until 300 years ago.
These days you're more likely to see a Shih Tzu outside the local
supermarket. This category is a selection of names that hark back to those
wilder times when wolves roamed and kings ruled.*

*Fun fact: the Irish word for 'wolf' is mac tíre,
meaning literally 'son of the land'.*

GIRLS' NAMES

Scáthach

Pronunciation: Skaw-hock

Known as 'the Shadow', Scáthach was a warrior and teacher from the Ulster Cycle, who trained Cú Chulainn in combat at her fortress, Dún Scáith, on the Isle of Skye. She passed on a deadly spear to him, the *gáe bulga*, which was made from the bones of a feared sea monster, the Curruid.

No record.

Badb

Pronunciation: Bav
Variation: Badhbh

Badb was the name of a war goddess who shapeshifted into a crow in order to help win battles for her family. She was one of three war-goddess sisters. Together, Badb, Macha and Anand were known as the 'Three Morrígan'.

No record.

Macha

Pronunciation: Mah-kah

Macha was another one of the three war goddesses, the Three Morrígan.

No record.

Áine

Pronunciation: Awn-ya
Variation: Enya

In Irish mythology Áine was the Queen of the Munster fairies and a wife of Fionn mac Cumhaill, the legendary warrior boy who first tasted the Salmon of Knowledge. In County Limerick, the hill of Knockainey (Cnoc Áine) is named after her.

Latest record: Áine ranked 117 with 40 newborns.
When records began: Aine ranked 133 with 36 newborns.

Clíodhna

Pronunciation: Klee-nah
Variations: Clíona, Cliona

Queen of the Banshees, a dark female ghost of the night. In Ireland, the howl of a fox can be confused with that of a banshee – or maybe the other way around ...

Latest record: Clíodhna ranked 213 with 20 newborns.
When records began: Cliona ranked 226 with 10 newborns.

Aisling

Pronunciation: Ash-ling
Variations: Ashling, Aislinn

In the Irish language the word *aisling* means 'dream' or 'vision'.

Latest record: Aisling ranked 154 with 30 newborns.
When records began: Aisling ranked 156 with 24 newborns.

Ciara

Pronunciation: Kee-rah

Ciara is closely related to the Irish word *ciar*, meaning 'of a dark complexion'. There's an anglicised version, 'Keira', like Keira Knightley. However, as there is no letter K in the Irish language, we're going to have to put our foot down.

Latest record: Ciara ranked 91 with 53 newborns.
When records began: Ciara ranked 146 with 26 newborns.

Lonán

Pronunciation: Lon-awn

Lon translates to 'blackbird' while *-án* means 'little'. While many cultures use the symbolism of blackbirds to mean death, Irish mythology tends to use these creatures to symbolise reincarnation and transformation.

No record.

Anu

Pronunciation: Ah-new

Anu was a goddess of nature, with a pair of mountains named after her in County Kerry. Named the Paps of Anu, these undulating hills are said to resemble her womanly figure.

No record.

Réaltín

Pronunciation: Rail-teen
Variations: Réiltín, Réailtín

This beautiful name comes from the word for 'star', *réalta*, and the diminutive *ín*, meaning 'little'. So if your daughter has an otherworldly presence or has come down from the heavens, perhaps Réaltín is the perfect name for her.

Latest record: Réaltín ranked 342 with 11 newborns.
When records began: No record.

Fiadh

Pronunciation: Fee-ah

Fiadh is the name everyone is talking about recently. It means 'wild deer' and 'respect' in Irish. It's come out of nowhere to become an extremely popular name for girls.

Latest record: Fiadh ranked 5 with 286 newborns.
When records began: No record.

Treasa

Pronunciation: Trass-ah

This name comes from the Irish words *treise* meaning 'strength' and *treas* meaning 'battle'. So if your little one is kicking up a storm in there, perhaps she is a Treasa.

No record.

Nóinín

Pronunciation: No-nyeen

This name means 'daisy' in Irish. Although there are plenty of daisies popping out of Irish soil, there isn't exactly an abundance of Nóiníns walking around these days. It's rare enough – which makes the name Nóinín as fresh as a daisy.

Latest record: Ranked 556 with 6 newborns.
When records began: No record.

Morrigan

Pronunciation: More-e-gone

The *Mór-ríoghán*, the 'great queen', was a shapeshifter of many forms, and she has many tales in Irish folklore. In what is the most well-known story, *The Cattle Raid of Cooley (Táin Bó Cúailnge)*, she appears to Cú Chulainn as no less than a beautiful young woman, an eel, a wolf and a cow before finally appearing as a raven to mark his death.

Latest record: Morrigan ranked 898 with 3 newborns.
When records began: No record.

BOYS' NAMES

Art

Pronunciation: Art

A much-forgotten Irish name, Art means 'bear' in old Irish. Much like its namesake, bears once inhabited Ireland, and while they're not coming back any time soon, a few more Arts would be nice.

Latest record: Art ranked 327 with 12 newborns.
When records began: No record.

Rónán

Pronunciation: Row-nan

Derived from the Irish word *rón*, meaning 'seal', Ronan translates to 'little seal' or 'seal person'. According to Irish legend, selkies – magical seals or mermaids – transform into humans when they swim too close to shore. Once in human form, they sometimes stay on land, marry, and have children who carry their seal ancestry, known as Ronans.

Latest record: Ronan ranked 65 with 88 newborns.
When records began: Ronan ranked 67 with 70 newborns.

Cathal

Pronunciation: Kah-al

Cathal comes from the Celtic words *cath*, meaning 'battle', and *fal*, meaning 'rule'.

Latest record: Cathal ranked 88 with 63 newborns.
When records began: Cathal ranked 96 with 32 newborns.

Oisín

Pronunciation: Ush-een

Oisín was the son of Ireland's most legendary figure, Fionn mac Cumhaill. Oisín was said to be the greatest poet in Ireland. The name means 'fawn' in honour of Oisín's mother, Sadhbh, who was turned into a deer by a treacherous druid.

Latest record: Oisín ranked 9 with 286 newborns.
When records began: Oisin ranked 232 with 3 newborns.

Éimhín

Pronunciation: Ay-veen

Éimhín means 'little swift one', coming from the old Irish word *eim*, meaning 'swift'. Nowadays, the name Evan is a popular version.

Latest record: Evan ranked 63 with 90 newborns.
When records began: No record.

Fionn

Pronunciation: Fyun
Variations: Fionnán, Finn

Most associated with Fionn mac Cumhaill, a warrior of Celtic mythology and an immortal guardian of the island of Ireland. It's no wonder that his second name is pronounced 'MacCool', as it is one of the coolest stories of Irish heritage. 'Finn' is the popular anglicised version.

Latest record: Fionn ranked 7 with 304 newborns.
When records began: No record.

Daithí

Pronunciation: Dah-hee

Daithí is said to have been the last pagan king of the whole island of Ireland.

Latest record: Daithí ranked 80 with 76 newborns.
When records began: No record.

Éanna

Pronunciation: Ain-a
Variation: Enda

Éanna was the name of many ancient Irish kings. Both strong and soft-sounding, it comes from the Irish word for 'bird', *éan*. It can be used as a unisex name, although it is most common among boys.

Latest record: Éanna ranked 112 with 49 newborns (boys) and was not recorded for girls.
When records began: Eanna ranked 327 with 4 newborns (girls). Enda ranked 75 with 49 newborns (boys).

Fionnbarra

Pronunciation: Fyun-bar-rah
Variations: Fionbharr, Finvarra, Finbarr

Fionbarra was the King of the *Daoine Sídhe (Aos Sí)*, a supernatural race of fairies in Celtic mythology. The name means 'the fair top'. Not actually referring to hair colour, but rather the top of a hill, the King of the Fairies.

Latest record: Finbarr ranked 785 with 3 newborns.
When records began: Finbarr ranked 70 with 61 newborns.

Luchta

Pronuncation: Lewk-tah
Variations: Luchtaine, Luachaid

Luchta was one of the three craftsmen gods, the *Trí Dé Dána*, who forged the weapons that the supernatural used in battle.

No record.

Balor

Pronunciation: Bah-lore

A bit of a bonkers name, Balor was the cyclops leader of the Fomorians, a band of supernatural malicious creatures. It is said that when he opened his eye he scorched the earth.

No record.

Cennétig

Pronunciation: Ken-ah-tig

Cennétig is the old Irish for 'ugly headed'. From this, we get the surname Cinnéidigh, anglicised as Kennedy. Despite its meaning, John F. Uglyhead went on to become America's most handsome president.

No record.

Conchobhar

Pronunciation: Kru-hoor
Variation: Conchubhair

The source of the name Conor and surname O'Connor. It is said to mean 'lover of wolves'. A great boy's name if you have a household of furry friends awaiting the newest member of the pack. It was very popular in the middle ages in Ireland. The name is still spelled using old Irish rules, so the pronunciation is not what you'd expect.

No record.

Conall

Pronunciation: Conn-ul
Variations: Conal, Conaill, Cunavalas (in Oghamic Irish)

Conall Cernach was a hero from the Ulster Cycle (one of the four major sagas in Irish mythology), described in *The Destruction of Da Derga's Hostel* as the fairest of Ireland's warriors. Conall's beauty might seem appealing – until you learn about his sleeping habits. Every night, he rested with the freshly severed head of a Connachtman tucked under his knee.

Latest record: Conall ranked 114 with 36 newborns.
When records began: Conal ranked 204 with 5 newborns.

Maolseachlann

Pronunciation: Mwail-shok-lan
Variations: Máel, Maele, Maelmura (nickname 'Othna')

The first syllable of this name, *maol*, means 'servant' but literally translates to 'bald', referring to the shaved heads of monks. 'Maolseachlann' has roots in some top characters from Irish history. In *The Voyage of Máel Dúin*, our hero sails from one strange island to another, encountering everything from colour-changing sheep to eternal laughter, and even a woman pelting nuts at him.

No record.

LOST
TREASURES

In this section, we delve into some of the oldest names that have graced this island: those of gods and warriors, which have sadly vanished from use. Often entirely missing from modern records, these Lost Treasures are longing to be rediscovered and to once again be heard ringing out across the land.

GIRLS' NAMES

Lasairíona

Pronunciation: Lassah-ree-nah
Variation: Lasairfhíona

Coming from the Irish words *lasair*, meaning 'flame', and *fíon*, meaning 'wine', this is a fiery name with some real vintage.

No record.

Béibhinn

Pronunciation: Bay-veen or Bay-vin
Variation: Béibhínn

Béibhinn was a goddess of the underworld. This name combines the meanings of the words 'woman' and 'melody', so this translates from old Irish to mean 'melodic woman'.

Latest record: Béibhinn ranked 441 with 8 newborns.
When records began: No record.

Maelíosa

Pronunciation: Mway-lee-sah

Maelíosa means 'servant of Jesus'. This is a particularly rare and beautiful sounding name.

No record.

Fiona

Pronunciation: Fee-oh-nah

Fiona means 'white' or 'fair'. *Fíon* also means wine in Irish. While the name has dropped in popularity recently, let's raise a glass to her comeback.

Latest record: Fiona ranked 556 with 6 newborns.
When records began: Fiona ranked 32 with 249 newborns.

Beith

Pronunciation: Beh

'Beith' comes from the letter 'B' in the Irish Ogham alphabet, and means 'birch tree'.

No record.

Danu

Pronunciation: Dah-noo
Variations: Dana, Danann

Danu is considered the mother goddess of Ireland. From this we get the Tuatha Dé Danann, meaning the 'Peoples of the Goddess Dana', a supernatural mythical race from pre-Christian Irish folklore.

Latest record: Danu ranked 736 with 4 newborns.
When records began: No record.

Bláithín

Pronunciation: Blaw-heen

This name comes from the Irish word for 'flower', *bláth*. Like in 'Róisín', again the '*-ín*' means 'little'. We're glad to see this name rising in the rankings, as it would be sad to see this 'little flower' face extinction.

Latest record: Bláithín ranked 121 with 38 newborns.
When records began: Blaithin ranked 332 with 4 newborns.

Mairéad

Pronunciation: Muh-raid
Variations: Mairead, Máiréad

Mairéad is a familiar Irish name that's disappeared in recent years. Its pet name Maisie is climbing the ranks instead and becoming rather popular in Ireland.

Latest record: Mairéad ranked 898 with 3 newborns.
When records began: Mairead ranked 115 with 47 newborns.

Seoidín

Pronunciation: Show-deen

This beautiful girl's name comes from the Irish word *seodra* meaning 'jewellery' and *ín*, which again means 'little'. She will be your little jewel.

Latest record: Seoidín ranked 181 with 25 newborns.
When records began: No record.

Nollaig

Pronunciation: Null-ig

Nollaig is the Irish word for Christmas. It is traditionally given to a baby as a middle name if he or she is born on Christmas Day, although for a brief period in the 1970s, it was a popular first name.

Latest record: Nollaig ranked 898 with 3 newborns.
When records began: No record.

Aifric

Pronunciation: Aff-rick

This name was very popular in Ireland from the eighth to tenth centuries and means 'pleasant' or 'freckled'. There are a lot of freckles in Ireland, so naturally this makes sense. What is surprising, however, is how rare the name has become one millennium later.

Latest record: Ranked 191 with 23 newborns.
When records began: No record.

Faoileann

Pronunciation: Fway-lin

Faoileann comes from the Irish word for 'fair maiden'. It's also very similar to the Irish word for seagull, *faoileán*, keh-kawww.

No record.

Líadan

Pronunciation: Lee-uh-din

Líadan comes from the Old Irish word *líath*, meaning 'grey'. Although 'grey girl' might initially seem a tad sombre, this meaning actually refers to the wisdom and knowledge that comes with aging gracefully. The name can be traced back at least to the seventh century, most notably to the poet Líadain of Corca Dhuibhne.

No record.

Damhnait

Pronunciation: Dov-nit or Dow-nit
Variations: Dymphna, Dympna, Davnet

From the Irish for 'ox', *damh*, this name means 'little calf'. Dympna had a brief appearance in the '60s and '70s with a handful of births, but apart from that, Damhnait and its variations are generally not found on records.

Latest record: No record.
When records began: Dympna ranked 109 with 53 newborns.

Étaín

Pronunciation: Aye-teen
Variation: Éadaoin

Étaín is the main character in one of Ireland's most bizarre stories, *The Wooing Of Étaín, Tochmarc Étaíne*. Considered to be the most beautiful woman in Ireland, Étaín is transformed by a jealous woman into a puddle of water and then into a purple fly, until finally being reborn as a baby 1,000 years later. It's a long story.

No record.

BOYS' NAMES

Cú

Pronunciation: Coo
Variation: Cúan (little hound)

Cú Chulainn is one of the most iconic heroes in Irish folklore, whose tales are too numerous to list here. Born Setanta, he earned the name Cú Chulainn as a child by killing Culann's guard dog in self-defence (in Old Irish *cú* means 'hound' or 'wolf') and offering to replace it until another could be raised, becoming the Hound of Culann.

Latest record: Cúan ranked 153 with 33 newborns.
When records began: No record.

Setanta

Pronunciation: Seh-tan-ta

Cú and Setanta are two names for the same person and we feel they're both deserving of their own place beside each other on this list.

Latest record: Setanta ranked 582 with 5 newborns.
When records began: No record.

Láeg

Pronunciation: Layg

Láeg was Cú Chulainn's best friend. While Láeg steered their chariot, Cú Chulainn sat shotgun and threw spears.

No record.

Conlaoch

Pronunciation: Con-layk
Variations: Connla, Conlaí

Conlaoch was the son of the legendary Cú Chulainn. His exploits feature in the 625-year-old manuscript *The Yellow Book of Lecan*, which can still be seen in Trinity College today.

No record.

Tuireann

Pronunciation: Tur-in
Variation: Tuirenn

The story *The Fate of the Children of Tuireann* (*Oidheadh Chloinne Tuireann*) originates from the era of the Tuatha Dé Danann. In this story, three brothers embark on a challenging quest, securing precious items through a blend of strategy, diplomacy and battle.

No record.

Ogma

Pronunciation: Og-mah

They say the pen is mightier than the sword, but for Ogma the chisel was stronger than the rock. This ancient demigod is said to have invented and carved script into stone. Thanks to Ogma, this island has its very own alphabet: Ogham.

No record.

Manann

Pronunciation: Mah-nan
Variations: Manannán, Manaunaun

The guardian of both the underworld and the sea in Irish mythology, Manann is linked to one of Ireland's most exquisite treasures – a delicate gold boat from the first century BC, which was part of the Broighter Hoard and can still be seen today in the National Museum of Ireland.

No record.

Fráech

Pronunciation: Fray-ack

Fráech looks particularly nice on paper. The name could also be shortened to simply Fráe. Legend has it he was a bit of a bad-arse. A defiant warrior and a hit with the ladies, he died only when defeated by a dragon.

No record.

Cumhall

Pronunciation: Cool
Variation: Cumhaill

There's no cooler name for your son. Cumhall was the leader of the Fianna, a band of warriors and the father of Fionn Mac Cumhaill, the main hero of the Fenian Cycle saga.

No record.

Tréanmhór

Pronunciation: Train-vor
Variation: Tréinmhór

Meaning 'great strength', in Irish mythology, Tréanmhór is one of the earlier figures and the grandfather of Fionn mac Cumhaill.

No record.

Ailill

Pronunciation: Al-yill

From the Irish *áilleacht*, meaning beauty. Ailill MacMáta was a King of Connacht and a husband of the legendary Queen Medb. He's best remembered for his role in the epic *Táin Bó Cúailnge*, where a marital spat over wealth sparked a cattle raid that engulfed Ireland in war.

No record.

Mel

Pronunciation: Mell
Variation: Mél

The name Mel itself is thought to be derived from the Old Irish word *maol*, meaning 'servant' or 'devotee', which is unsurprising considering Saint Mel was likely a nephew of Saint Patrick's, who accompanied him to Ireland. This name also works for a baby girl.

Latest record: No record.
When records began: Mel ranked 129 with 16 newborns (boys).

Cathair

Pronunication: Kah-er

Another with the spirit of a warrior, this name comes from the Irish *cath*, meaning 'battle' or 'war'. Catháir Mór (the great Catháir) was killed in battle by Conn, so if you already have a boy called Conn, best keep an eye on them.

No record.

Nuadha

Pronunciation: New-ah-dah
Variation: Núadu

Núadu means 'hero', and he was a warrior famed for having a silver arm, after losing his own in battle. The Tandragee Idol, a 3,000-year-old sandstone carved figure, still sits in Saint Patrick's Cathedral, Armagh; in 1961, an art historian boldly claimed that the statue was Núadu, even though the sculpture predates the first writings of him by about 2,000 years. Talk about going out on a limb.

No record.

Bres

Pronunciation: Bress

The king who succeeded Núadu was Bres the Beautiful. Bres was born of two worlds: the Fomorians (giant sea people) and the Tuatha Dé Danann. Deposed for being a poor king, he redeemed himself by teaching the Tuatha Dé Danann the secrets of seasonal farming, and how to rear cows that produced endless milk.

No record.

Samhain

Pronunciation: Sow-in
Variations: Samuin and Samain

Halloween does indeed come from Ireland and was first known as the festival of Samhain over 2,000 years ago. Samhain represents a time of year, at the end of summer and the beginning of winter, when the boundary between this world and the Otherworld is believed to be thinnest, allowing spirits to pass through. A frightfully good name for your little monster.

No record.

Éibhear

Pronunciation: Ave-er
Variations: Éber, Heber

Éibhear is a name that's as hard as stone, coming from the Irish word for granite, *eibhear*. It is commonly anglicised to Heber or Ivor.

No record.

Dealán

Pronunciation: Dah-lawnn
Variation: Déaglán

Dealán comes from the Irish word gealán, meaning a 'gleam' or a 'bright spell'.

No record.

Feardorcha

Pronunciation: Far-dorkh-ah

Feardorcha is a clear combination of the Irish words for 'man', *fear*, and 'dark', *dorcha*. In Irish mythology, the story behind the name isn't much brighter. Fear Doirich was a druid who turned Sadhbh into a deer for rejecting him, but Fionn mac Cumhaill's hounds recognised her as human and broke the spell, and they married. This is probably where the story should end, but Feardorcha turned her back into a deer and she was never seen again.

No record.

Fachtna

Pronunciation: Fack-nah

This name has an undeniably punchy, old-world charm. The most famous bearer was Fáthach, a High King of Ireland roughly 50 to 100 years before the birth of Jesus. Today, Fachtna is barely making an appearance on birth records. Is the name too bold for a baby? Fack-nah! Bring it back.

Latest record: No record.
When records began: Ranked 232 with 3 newborns.

NAMES
from IRISH MYTHOLOGY

Ireland has a rich tapestry of myths and legends, passed down through the ages. We're an island of storytellers, so Irish heritage stretches back to the time when heroes journeyed across the land and magical creatures roamed freely. Much of Irish identity is rooted in these mythological characters - many of whom have pretty fantastic names.

GIRLS' NAMES

Brigid

Pronunciation: Bridge-id
Variations: Bridget, Bríd, Breege, Breda

For most Irish people, the name Brigid will bring to mind the Saint Brigid's Cross. The cross is made from woven straw or rushes and hung on doors to keep bad spirits at bay. The name dates back to pre-Christian Ireland, where Brigid was a goddess and member of Tuatha Dé Danann. The Christians knew a good character when they heard one and converted her into the Mother Saint of Ireland.

Latest record: Brigid ranked 736 with 4 newborns.
When records began: Brigid ranked 29 with 272 newborns.

Eimear

Pronunciation: Ee-mur
Variation: Emer

Eimear, the wife of the hero Cú Chulainn, is celebrated in Irish mythology for her 'six gifts of womanhood'. These qualities – strength, beauty, a gentle voice, wisdom, skill in needlework, and generosity – are said to have enchanted Cú Chulainn, making her one of the most admired women in Irish legend.

Latest record: Eimear ranked 294 with 14 newborns.
When records began: Eimear ranked 302 with 5 newborns.

Sadhbh

Pronunciation: Sive (rhymes with 'hive')
Variation: Saibh

In Irish mythology Sadhbh is a well-known figure who was twice turned into a deer by a wicked druid for refusing his advances. She chose Fionn mac Cumhaill instead and had their child Oisín, the great poet, whose name means 'little deer'.

Latest record: Sadhbh ranked 38 with 117 newborns.
When records began: No record.

Cáit

Pronunciation: Cawtch

Cáit is a rare fairy creature in Irish mythology, a wild black cat with a white spot on her chest.

Latest record: Cáit ranked 441 with 8 newborns.
When records began: No record.

Ethniu

Pronunciation: Eth-new
Variations: Eithne, Ethliu, Ethlinn, Ethna, Ethel, Enya

Madly enough, in Irish mythology Ethniu was the daughter of the supernatural cyclops, Balor. Ethniu was known for her beauty and is a good example of how in Ireland, no matter the face of the father, it's possible to have a beautiful daughter.

Latest record: No record.
When records began: Eithne ranked 126 with 41 newborns.

Deichtine

Pronunciation: Jeh-tinna

Tumbling down the tree of Irish mythology, we come across Deichtine, the mother of the fearless Irish warrior Cú Chulainn.

No record.

Fódhla

Pronunciation: Foe-la
Variations: Fódla, Fóla

Fódhla was a goddess in Irish mythology. One of the Tuatha Dé Danann, she had two sisters, Banba and Ériu. The three sisters asked a bard that the land of Ireland be named after them. Ériu is the early form of Éire, so it's safe to say her sister won that fight. Nonetheless, Fódhla is still considered a poetic name for Ireland.

Latest record: Fódhla ranked 197 with 22 newborns.
When records began: No record.

Banbha

Pronunciation: Ban-vah
Variation: Banba

While Ireland would be named after her sister Ériu, according to an ancient Irish folktale, Banbha gets the bragging right of being the first person to set foot on the island of Ireland. She was a matron goddess of Ireland.

No record.

Fionnuala

Pronunciation: Fin-oola
Variation: Fionnghuala

Fionnuala means 'white-shouldered', conveying an image of long, flowing fair hair. In the legend of the Children of Lir, Fionnuala and her siblings were transformed into swans for 900 years by their evil stepmother. Like her wicked spell, this name is both captivating and enchanting. A popular name in the past, Fionnuala has dropped off significantly in recent times.

Latest record: No record.
When records began: Fionnuala ranked 135 with 34 newborns.

Dearbhla

Pronunciation: Der-vla

Variations: Dearbhfhorghaill, Deirbhile, Derbáil and Dervla

Dearbhla means 'daughter of destiny'. The name also echoes the Lia Fáil, the Stone of Destiny, still standing at the Hill of Tara, where ancient kings were crowned until 500 AD.

Latest record: Dearbhla ranked 898 with 3 newborns.
When records began: No record.

Ailbhe

Pronunciation: Al-va

In Irish mythology Ailbhe was one of Ireland's greatest female warriors. She was also known for her freckled cheeks. This name likely comes from the Irish word *aolmhach*, meaning 'lime-white'. While Ailbhe is usually a girl's name, Saint Ailbe of Emly was a male saint, known as 'the other Saint Patrick', who's said to have converted the south of Ireland during the same period in which Saint Patrick was alive.

Latest record: Ailbhe ranked 65 with 83 newborns (girls) and was not recorded for boys.
When records began: Ailbhe ranked 372 with 3 newborns (girls) and was not recorded for boys.

BOYS' NAMES

Lugh

Pronunciation: Loo
Variations: Lú, Lug, Lugnasad (the first day of August)

Lug was a warrior god in Celtic mythology, who was amazing at pretty much everything. Not a jack of all trades but a master; from the fine arts to the art of war, he was revered for his skills with a spear.

Latest record: Lugh ranked 785 with 3 newborns.
When records began: No record.

Dagda

Pronunciation: Dag-dah

The Dagda is considered the top god in Irish mythology as the chief god of the Tuatha Dé Danann. He was a giant who dragged his magical club around the landscape, forming Ireland's ditches.

No record.

Bodhbh

Pronunciation: Boev
Variations: Bodb, Bove, Bodhbh

Bodhbh is the eldest son of The Dagda. This old Irish name is associated with Bodb Derg, who went on to be the king of the Tuatha Dé Danann and the king of the *síde* – or fairy folk – of Munster, who lived underground.

No record.

Aengus

Pronunciation: En-gus
Variation: Óengus

Aengus was another son of The Dagda. The name Aengus is associated with the winter solstice illumination of Newgrange, symbolising the rebirth of the sun and the cyclical nature of life and death.

Latest record: No record.
When records began: Aengus ranked 204 with 5 newborns.

Miach

Pronunciation: Mee-uck

Miach was a grandson of the The Dagda. He was known as a healer who surpassed even the skills of the god of healing, his father Dian Cécht. It is said that from his grave, all the healing herbs of Ireland have grown.

No record.

Aed

Pronunciation: Aid
Variations: Aodh, Aedan

Aed is most typically associated with fire and is the Lord of the Underworld. A great name for a baby with a fiery head of red hair.

Latest record: Aodh ranked 584 with 5 newborns.
When records began: Aodh ranked 191 with 6 newborns.

Tethra

Pronunciation: Cheh-rah

Tethra was an ancient warrior of the Fomorians, fiercest rivals of the Tuatha Dé Danann. His sword retained memories.

No record.

Cermait

Pronunciation: Ker-mit

No, not the frog. One of the more promiscuous and well-endowed Irish figures. He had a good run before being murdered by Lug's wife for revealing too much of himself.

No record.

Abhartach

Pronunciation: Aw-var-tock
Variations: Abartach, Avartagh

Abhartach was a wicked dwarf from the North of Ireland who kept rising from the grave until a druid advised burying him upside down. Later tales say he drank blood, sparking theories he inspired Bram Stoker's *Dracula*. His grave, now called 'The Giant's Grave', still stands in County Derry, marked by stones under a hawthorn tree.

No record.

Conn

Pronunciation: Con

This name means 'head', or 'knowledge', in Irish. One of Ireland's High Kings was known as Conn of the Hundred Battles; this child might have to be removed from a few playground scraps.

Latest record: Conn ranked 150 with 34 newborns.
When records began: No record.

Domhnall

Pronunciation: Doe-nal
Variations: Dónal, Donald

Domhnall is a strong name that was given to no fewer than five High Kings of Ireland, each of whom ruled the entire island at one stage. Befitting of these High Kings, the name means 'world ruler'.

Latest record: Domhnall ranked 430 with 8 newborns.
When records began: Donal ranked 45 with 144 newborns. Donald ranked 104 with 27 newborns.

Fiachra

Pronunciation: Fee-ah-kra
Variations: Fiacra, Fiach, Fiacre

The Irish word for 'raven' is *fiach*, a bird that comes up time and again in Irish mythology. Fiachra was also one of the four children of Lir as well as a King of Munster.

Latest record: Fiachra ranked 123 with 45 newborns.
When records began: Fiach ranked 249 with 3 newborns. Fiacre ranked 262 with 3 newborns.

Naoise

Pronunciation: Nee-sha
Variations: Naisi, Noíse

In Irish mythology, Naoise was a famed hunter and warrior. He was the nephew of King Conchobhar, who married Deirdre. Nowadays it is used for both girls and boys.

Latest record: Naoise ranked 123 with 37 newborns (girls) and 162 with 31 newborns (boys).
When records began: No record.

Elatha

Pronunciation: Eh-la-tah

Elatha was a king of the Fomorians, the enemies of Ireland's first settlers and rival supernatural race the Tuatha Dé Danann. Elatha is also sometimes considered the goddess of the moon, making this another lovely unisex name.

No record.

Ferdia

Pronunciation: Fur-dee-ah
Variation: Fer Diadh

We will end with poor Ferdia, who died at the hands of his friend Cú Chulainn in the most uncomfortable way. During the epic Cattle Raid of Cooley *(Táin Bó Cúailnge)*, Cú Chulainn threw his spear at Ferdia's rear end, fatally wounding him. The unfortunate tale of Ireland's Achilles' Arse.

Latest record: Ferdia ranked 472 with 7 newborns.
When records began: No record.

NAMES
by GEOGRAPHY

Many places in Ireland provide monikers for children. From central sites in Ireland's history such as the consecrated Hill of Tara, where all-Ireland kings were crowned, to remote locations like the Aran Islands, we find great names throughout. In this section, we travel around Ireland picking up a few gems from its geography.

GIRLS' NAMES

Gobnait

Pronunciation: Gawb-nit
Variation: Goibniu

According to local legend, Saint Gobnait protected her abbey from a group of raiders when she unleashed her bees on them. Her church can still be found on the Aran island of Inis Oírr. This tiny ruin from the eleventh century is said to contain the remains of Gobnait's beehive hut.

Today, there's even an annual event for people with the name Gobnait. If you find yourself in Ballyvourney, County Cork on 11 February, you'll witness all the living Gobnaits of Ireland hanging out together on a day called 'The Gathering of Gobnaits'.

Latest record: No record.
When records began: Gobnait ranked 300 with 5 newborns.

Tara

Pronunciation: Tah-rah

The name Tara is associated with the Hill of Tara, the ancient ceremonial site in County Meath. It was the inauguration location for all the High Kings of Ireland and now contains the Standing Stone of Destiny, the Lia Fáil.

Latest record: Tara ranked 171 with 26 newborns.
When records began: Tara ranked 327 with 4 newborns.

Boann

Pronunciation: Bawn

Boann was the Irish goddess of the River Boyne – the very river where the Salmon of Knowledge was caught by Fionn mac Cumhaill, gifting him all the knowledge of the world.

No record.

Clodagh

Pronunciation: Clow-dah

Clodagh flows as freely as the river it is named after; the River Clodiagh in County Waterford.

Latest record: Clodagh ranked 42 with 109 newborns.
When records began: Clodagh ranked 149 with 25 newborns.

Laoise

Pronunciation: Lee-sha

This name is similar to the name of County Laois. In Irish, it's likely the name is derived from *lóeg*, which has a figurative meaning of 'favourite' or 'darling' and a literal meaning of 'young deer'.

Latest record: Laoise ranked 98 with 48 newborns.
When records began: No record.

Clara

Pronunciation: Clah-rah
Variation: Claragh

Clara is an Anglicisation of the Latin name Clarus meaning 'bright'. Coincidently, it is also very close to the Irish word *clár*, which means a 'flat plain'; an apt description for County Clare's UNESCO World Heritage Site, the Burren. The name could also relate to the town of Clara, whose lesser-known bog almost won a prestigious UNESCO World Heritage Site but was 'bogged down' in technicalities.

Latest record: Clara ranked 65 with 83 newborns.
When records began: Clara ranked 329 with 4 newborns.

Orlaith

Pronunciation: Or-la
Variations: Orla, Orlaith, Órfhlaith

Orla comes from the Irish word for 'gold', *ór*, and 'ruler', *flaith*. Put them together and you've got yourself a little golden princess.

Latest record: Orlaith ranked 372 with 10 newborns.
When records began: Orla ranked 52 with 120 newborns.

Saorlaith

Pronunciation: Sare-lah
Variations: Saorla and Saorfhlaith

Saorlaith, albeit close to Orlaith, is a name in its own right, meaning 'free-born princess' or 'noble princess'.

Latest record: Saorlaith ranked 259 with 16 newborns
When records began: No record.

Ness

Pronunciation: Ness
Variations: Neasa, Nessa

No, nothing to do with any Scottish lake monsters. Ness played an important part in Irish mythology. She was a Princess of Ulaid, a part of Ireland which would eventually be known as Ulster. She was the mother of Conchobhar Mac Nessa, a King of Ulster.

Latest record: Nessa ranked 307 with 18 newborns.
When records began: Nessa ranked 300 with 5 newborns.

Úna

Pronunciation: Oo-nah
Variations: Oonagh, Onagh, Una

Úna was a fairy queen of western Ireland and wife of Finvarra. This supernatural couple of the Tuatha Dé Danann are said to sometimes live inside a fairy hill in Cnoc Meadha, County Galway. In the Irish language today, *uan* means 'lamb'. This name ticks all the boxes: simplicity, soft sound, and a strong connection to mythology and the Irish language.

Latest record: Úna ranked 307 with 13 newborns.
When records began: Una ranked 87 with 70 newborns.

Ériu

Pronunciation: Air-ew

Éire, the Irish word for Ireland, comes directly from the Old Irish name *Ériu*, who was the sovereignty goddess of Ireland. Her name is rooted in meanings like 'earth,' 'soil', and 'place of abundance', symbolising the very essence of the land. Not just *an* Irish name, but *the* Irish name.

Latest record: Ériu ranked 441 with 8 newborns.
When records began: No record.

BOYS' NAMES

Brú

Pronunciation: Brew

Brú means 'palace' and is also associated with Brú na Bóinne, the World Heritage Site along the River Boyne. Ireland's richest archaeological landscape, it features the prehistoric passage tombs of Newgrange, Knowth and Dowth, dating back over 5,000 years ago. These Neolithic structures contain one of the largest collections of megalithic art in Europe.

No record.

Aran

Pronunciation: Ar-un
Variations: Arran, Árón

Taylor Swift's favourite jumper. The three Aran islands are known for their cold winters on the wild Atlantic, conditions which led to the invention of these lovely woolly sweaters.

Latest record: Aran ranked 302 with 13 newborns.
When records began: No record.

Tieve

Pronunciation: Tehv

Tieve comes from the Irish word for 'hillside', *taobh*. If you choose this name, you might want to bring your son to explore the 400-metre-high mountain which is associated with this name, Tievebulliagh in Northern Ireland. On this mountain, ancient axe heads have been found so large that it remains unclear if they were really used or rather were for ceremonial purposes.

No record.

Tyrone

Pronunciation: Tie-rone

In the Irish language, Tyrone means Eoghan's land, or Tír Eoghan. It is also one of Ireland's great Gaelic football counties.

No record.

Turlach

Pronunciation: Tur-loch
Variations: Turlough, Tarlach

A strong Irish name. In the Irish language a *turlach* is a lake that dries up in the summer or disappears over limestone. Lord Turlough O'Donnell was one of Ireland's more virile men. In 1423, he had 18 sons with 10 different women.

Latest record: Turlough ranked 582 with 5 newborns.
When records began: No record.

Cainneach

Pronunciation: Can-yach

Coming from the Irish word *caoin*, meaning 'gentle' and 'kind', this name had a particular connection to County Kilkenny. Saint Cainneach of Aghaboe is the patron saint of Kilkenny and his impressive bust can be found in the city. While it is more common as a male name, there are records of it being used as a female name. Cainneach was a daughter of a High King.

No record.

Tulach

Pronunciation: Tull-uck
Variation: Tully

Tullamore, a town in the heart of Ireland famous for its whiskey distillery, takes its name from the Irish *tulach* and *mór*, meaning 'mound' and 'big'. Some whiskey connoisseurs like a tipple of Tullamore Dew so much, we are even hearing of Tully outside the pub now.

No record.

Senan

Pronunciation: Sen-nan
Variation: Seanán

Senan means 'little wise one' and is linked to Saint Senn of Scattery Island, which lies off the coast of County Clare. This saint was a key figure in early Christianity, celebrated for his deep wisdom. For this reason, the name Senan symbolises a person of great knowledge, often turned to for counsel and direction. The name has seen an explosion in popularity in recent years.

Latest record: Senan ranked 59 with 99 newborns.
When records began: Senan ranked 191 with 6 newborns.

Lórcán

Pronunciation: Lore-kawn
Variation: Lorcan

A classic Irish name, Lorcan means 'little fierce one'. It can be dated back to the twelfth century, when the patron saint of Dublin, Saint Lorcan O'Toole, served as an important mediator in negotiations between the Norman invaders and the native Irish.

Latest record: Lorcan ranked 137 with 38 newborns.
When records began: Lorcan ranked 147 with 11 newborns.
Lórcán: No record.

Innis

Pronunciation: Inn-iss

While no man is an island, they may be an Innis. This name literally means 'island'.

No record.

Iarlaith

Pronunciation: Ear-lah
Variations: Iarlaithe, Iarla, Jarlath

From the old Irish word *flaith*, which means 'leader' or 'lord'. It's believed there was a priest, Iarlaithe Mac Loga, who founded the monastic School of Tuam, which attracted scholars from around the country. It can be used as a boys' or girls' name.

Latest record: Iarlaith ranked 99 with 56 newborns (boys).
When records began: No record.

POPULAR IRISH
names TODAY

In this section, we've gone through the most popular Irish baby names today, skipping over a few of the Anglo-American names and focusing on the more traditional ones.

Hopefully, this gives you some inspiration for names that are well liked at the moment.

GIRLS' NAMES

Éabha

Pronunciation: Ay-vah

Coming from the story of Adam and Eve. Éabha means Eve, signifying the human race, *Síol Éabha.*

Latest record: Éabha ranked 2 with 293 newborns.
When records began: No record.

Alannah

Pronunciation: Ah-lah-nah

A little on the nose, this name, Alannah literally comes from the Irish word for child, *leanbh.*

Latest record: Alannah ranked 117 with 40 newborns.
When records began: No record.

Croía

Pronunciation: Kree-ah
Variations: Críoa, Croia, Croíadh

Croía comes from the Irish word *croí*, meaning 'heart'. A perfect name for a baby that will steal yours.

Latest record: Croía ranked 16 with 188 newborns.
When records began: No record.

Cara

Pronunciation: Cah-rah

Cara means 'friend' in Irish; however, its origins are rather universal, as similar variations of this name are also found in Italy, Germany, Greece and beyond. *'A stór, mo chara.'* My treasure, my friend.

Latest record: Cara ranked 37 with 118 newborns.
When records began: No record.

Máire

Pronunciation: Moy-rah
Variations: Maire, Maura, Mary, Móra

Mary was the most popular baby name in Ireland when records began. It's since become a lot less typical. So if you're wondering what to call your little lamb, then why not Máire?

Latest record: Mary ranked 105 with 46 newborns.
When records began: Maire ranked 113 with 48 newborns.

Hazel

Pronunciation: Hay-zel

Hazel is a name linked to creativity and wisdom. The hazel tree *(crann coill)* features in the famous Irish story of the Salmon of Knowledge. The fish gained worldly wisdom from having eaten nine hazelnuts that fell into the Well of Wisdom *(Tobar Segais)*. The name also has its own Irish letter, linked to the letter 'C', which is one vertical line with four horizontal lines to the left. (See the Ogham alphabet chart for the image.)

Latest record: Hazel ranked 44 with 108 newborns.
When records began: Hazel ranked 154 with 24 newborns.

Doireann

Pronunciation: Dir-in

Doireann has deep roots in the Irish language. The Irish word *doire* means 'oak wood' or 'grove'.

Latest record: Doireann ranked 171 with 26 newborns.
When records began: No record.

Éala

Pronunciation: Ail-ah
Variation: Ayla

Éala, just a fada away from the Irish word for swan, *eala* – a creature that comes up in many Irish myths. In the Children of Lir, Lir's four children were turned into swans for 900 years by their jealous stepmother.

Latest record: Éala ranked 40 with 114 newborns.
When records began: No record.

Cadhla

Pronunciation: Kye-lah

Cadhla was originally a boys' name meaning handsome, but it has risen in the ranks among popular girls' names and is now taken to mean 'beautiful'.

Latest record: Cadhla ranked 116 with 41 newborns.
When records began: No record.

Cora

Pronunciation: Core-ah

Cora is associated with the Irish word for 'justice', *cóir*. *An chóir a dhéanamh* means 'to do what is just and proper'.

Latest record: Cora ranked 77 with 66 newborns.
When records began: Cora ranked 145 with 27 newborns.

Nora

Pronunciation: Nore-ah
Variations: Onóra, Norah, Nóirín

Nora is found within the Irish word *onórach*, which means 'honourable'. The name Nora is also associated with Bloomsday, as Nora Barnacle was the muse and wife of Irish author James Joyce. Their first romantic outing on 16 June 1904 is now celebrated as Bloomsday, the day on which Joyce's novel *Ulysses* takes place.

Latest record: Nora ranked 84 with 61 newborns.
When records began: Nora ranked 30 with 264 newborns.

Síofra

Pronunciation: Shee-frah

In Irish *síofra* means 'elf', 'fairy', 'changeling' or 'precocious child'. With this name, you've got your child's characteristics covered, whether they're top of the class or away with the fairies.

Latest record: Síofra ranked 98 with 48 newborns.
When records began: No record.

Siún

Pronunciation: Shoon

Siún in Irish literally means 'confused' or 'exhausted'. Let's face it, most babies *are* tired and confused.

Latest record: Siún ranked 149 with 31 newborns.
When records began: No record.

Muireann

Pronunciation: Mwir-in

Muireann means 'white sea', coming from the Irish word for 'sea', *muir*. In Irish mythology, Muirne was the mother of Fionn mac Cumhaill.

Latest record: Muireann ranked 171 with 26 newborns.
When records began: No record.

Aoibhinn

Pronunciation: Aiv-een

As with the name Aoibhe, this name comes from the Irish root word *aoibh*, meaning 'beauty'.

Latest record: Aoibhinn ranked 412 with 9 newborns.
When records began: No record.

Kathleen

Pronunciation: Cat-lean
Variations: Cathleen, Caitlyn, Katelyn

While Kathleen, or its variations such as Katelyn, may sound originally Irish, this name actually comes from ancient Greek and the adjective *kataros*, meaning 'pure'.

Nonetheless it's deeply woven its way into Irish culture. Kathleen Ni Houlihan is a literary figure used by Ireland's best-loved writers such as Yeats as the personification of an Irish woman, telling young men to go off and fight for Ireland's cause.

Latest record: Kathleen ranked 197 with 22 newborns.
When records began: Kathleen ranked 23 with 301 newborns.

Síomha

Pronunciation: Shee-u-vah
Variation: Síthmaith

Síomha, comes from the Irish words *síth*, meaning 'peace', and *maith*, meaning 'good'.

Latest record: Síomha ranked 166 with 28 newborns.
When records began: No record.

Rioghnach

Pronunciation: Ree-an-ock
Variation: Ríona

A name that comes from the Irish word *ríonaigh*, meaning 'queen'.

No record.

Bronagh

Pronunciation: Bro-nah
Variations: Brónach, Brona

Bronagh means 'sorrow'. Legend has it that Saint Brónach hung a bell in a young tree that was discovered a thousand years later during the Night of the Big Wind in 1839.

Latest record: Bronagh ranked 307 with 13 newborns.
When records began: Brona ranked 274 with 6 newborns.

Eibhlín

Pronunciation: Eye-lean
Variations: Eibhlin, Eileen, Eibhilín

Yet another name to mean beauty. This time, from the Old Irish word *oíph* meaning 'radiant', and ending with *-ín*, this name means 'little beauty'.

Latest record: Eibhlín ranked 504 with 7 newborns.
When records began: Eibhlin ranked 372 with 3 newborns.

Laragh

Pronunciation: Lah-rah

Laragh is associated with the Irish word *láithreach* meaning 'the site' or 'ruins of a building'. It's also a town in County Wicklow.

Latest record: Laragh ranked 631 with 5 newborns.
When records began: No record.

Dáire

Pronunciation: Dah-rah
Variation: Dara

Dáire is associated with a letter from the Irish Ogham Alphabet, where D is for *dair*, the mighty oak tree.

Latest record: Dáire ranked 631 with 5 newborns.
When records began: Daire ranked 191 with 6 newborns.

BOYS' NAMES

Seán

Pronunciation: Shawn
Variation: Sean

The top boy's name in 2024 was Jack. The Irish version of Jack is Seán, meaning 'gift from God'.

Latest record: Seán ranked 15 with 222 newborns.
When records began: Sean ranked 38 with 171 newborns.

Nóe

Pronunciation: No-ah

The second most popular boy's name of 2024 was Noah. The Irish equivalent is Nóe. Nóe derives from the Hebrew word meaning 'rest' or 'comfort'. So if your baby is fond of a nap, maybe he's a little Nóe. This is a very rare name in Irish, and is also unisex. Per year, only one or two children in Ireland are named Nóe.

No record.

Rían

Pronunciation: Ree-inn
Variations: Rian, Riain, Riaan, Ryan

Ryan is a popular name nowadays, which in Irish is Riain. It comes from the Irish words *rí*, meaning 'king', and *rian*, meaning 'direction'. A name that will set your little one on his path to greatness.

Latest record: Rían ranked 3 with 432 newborns.
When records began: No record.

Séamus

Pronunciation: Shay-mus

Variations: Seamus, Séamas, Shaymus, Sheamus, Shamus

The fifth most popular boy's name of 2024 was James, meaning 'usurper'. The Irish version is Séamus, which Irish people like to playfully name their second-born. James is also the most popular baby name in the US over the last hundred years.

Latest record: Séamus ranked 125 with 44 newborns.
When records began: Seamus ranked 60 with 87 newborns.

Cillian

Pronunciation: Killy-in

Cillian comes from the Irish word *cillín*, which means 'little church'.

Latest record: Cillian ranked 4 with 352 newborns.
When records began: No record.

Conor

Pronunciation: Con-er

Conor is an all-time favourite Irish name. Behind this name is the meaning 'lover of wolves'. Conaire Mór (meaning Conor the Great) was a High King of Ireland in pre-Christian times. It is said that he ruled peacefully for up to 70 years, during the period of Jesus Christ.

Latest record: Conor ranked 19 with 210 newborns.
When records began: Conor ranked 56 with 97 newborns.

Ádam

Pronunciation: Aw-dum
Variation: Ádhamh

According to a well-known publication, Adam is a good name for a firstborn. It means 'the earth'. The Irish variation on this name sees a fada appear on the first, giving us Ádam.

Latest record: Adam ranked 25 with 188 newborns.
When records began: No record.

Liam

Pronunciation: Lee-am
Variation: Uilliam

A strong Irish name for a boy. Liams are protectors. Liam is a shortened version of the old Germanic Willhelm, which means 'helmet of will'.

Latest record: Liam ranked 8 with 303 newborns.
When records began: Liam ranked 54 with 111 newborns.

Darragh

Pronunciation: Da-ra
Variations: Darach, Daire, Doire, Dara

Darragh comes from the Old Irish word *daire* (modern Irish *doire*), which means 'oak'. The Dara Knot is also a classic Celtic design. It is a symbol, which comes in many variations, of an intertwined knot that resembles tree roots.

Latest record: Darragh ranked 26 with 184 newborns.
When records began: No record.

Mícheál

Pronunciation: Mee-hall

Mícheál is Michael in Irish. One of Ireland's most well-known founding fathers was Michael Collins. Back in 1964 Michael was the third most popular name in Ireland.

Latest record: Mícheál ranked 252 with 17 newborns.
1964: Michael ranked 3 with 2157 newborns.

Tomás

Pronunciation: Tuh-maws

Thomas is an Aramaic name meaning 'twin', the Irish version of which is Tomás.

Latest record: Tomás ranked 81 with 73 newborns.
When records began: Tomas ranked 181 with 7 newborns.

Patrick

Pronunciation: Pah-trick

Typically shortened to 'Paddy', even in Ireland. This name was the second most popular baby name when records began in 1964. If your son is born on 17 March, or you hate snakes, then this might be a good name for him. Despite being the patron saint of Ireland, Saint Patrick was born to a Roman family in what is now Wales. The name Patrick comes from the early medieval Patricias, meaning 'of the Patrician [or aristocratic] class'.

Latest record: Patrick ranked 16 with 220 newborns.
When records began: Patrick ranked 2 with 2,235 newborns.

Páidí

Pronunciation: Paw-dee

Páidí, the Irish pet name for Patrick, has vastly overtaken its original version in popularity – earning its own spot on this list.

Latest record: Páidí ranked 22 with 201 newborns.
When records began: No record.

Caolán

Pronunciation: Kway-lawn
Variation: Caelan

Caolán comes from the Irish word *caol,* meaning 'slender'. The spelling variation 'Caelan' is popular recently.

Latest record: Caelan ranked 43 with 128 newborns.
When records began: No records.

Tiernan

Pronunciation: Tear-nin

A common enough surname, Tiernan is now finding popularity as a first name. It comes from the Irish word for 'lord', *tiarna*.

Latest record: Tiernan ranked 109 with 51 newborns.
When records began: Tiernan ranked 235 with 3 newborns.

Cuán

Pronunciation: Coo-awn
Variation: Cú

Cuán comes from the Irish word *cú*, meaning 'hound', and has earned its own spot on this list due to its rising popularity.

Latest record: Cuán ranked 153 with 33 newborns.
When records began: No record.

Faolán

Pronunciation: Fway-lawn

Faolán is yet another Irish name that means 'little wolf'. Safe to say, this apex predator of ancient Ireland continues to leave a lasting impression.

Latest record: Faolán ranked 174 with 29 newborns.
When records began: No record.

Bearnárd

Pronunciation: Bar-nawrd

Bernard in Irish is Bearnárd. This is a name that came to Ireland with the Normans and means 'as strong as a bear'.

Latest record: Bernard ranked 582 with 5 newborns.
When records began: Bernard ranked 33 with 201 newborns.

León

Pronunciation: Lee-own

León comes from from the Latin for 'lion', not that you'll find any of those in Ireland – outside of Dublin Zoo, anyway.

Latest record: Leon ranked 60 with 93 newborns.
When records began: No record.

Dáithí

Pronunciation: Dah-hee
Variation: Daithí

A spritely name, Dáithí comes from the Irish word *daithe*, meaning 'swiftness'.

Latest record: Dáithí ranked 80 with 76 newborns.
When records began: No records.

Breandán

Pronunciation: Bran-dawn
Variation: Brendan

Brendan of Birr was also one of the Twelve Apostles of Ireland. Brendan means 'prince' or 'king', from the old Welsh *breenhin*.

Latest record: Brendan ranked 394 with 9 newborns.
When records began: Brendan ranked 17 with 426 newborns.

Oscar

Pronunciation: Oss-cur
Variation: Osgur

Oscar was one of Ireland's mythical sons in the Fenian cycle. This name comes from the Irish words for 'deer', *os*, and 'friend', *car*.

Latest record: Oscar ranked 32 with 159 newborns.
When records began: No record.

Colm

Pronunciation: Coh-lum
Variation: Colum

Colm in Irish means 'dove'. This name was kept popular in Ireland due to Saint Colmcille, who was one of the trinity of Ireland's patron saints, along with Saint Patrick and Saint Brigid.

Latest record: Colm ranked 350 with 11 newborns.
When records began: Colm ranked 45 with 144 newborns.

Logan

Pronunciation: Low-gun

Logan means 'a sheltered valley in the woods'.

Latest record: Logan ranked 86 with 66 newborns.
When records began: No record.

Aodhán

Pronunciation: Ay-dawn
Variation: Aidan

Aodhán means 'little fire', coming from the Old Irish word for fire, *aodh*. Aodhán Mac Gabhráin was a first-century Celtic king, ruling an area of Ireland and Scotland known as Dál Riata.

Latest record: Aodhán ranked 231 with 19 newborns.
When records began: No record.

Caoimhín

Pronunciation: Kwee-veen

Kevin is actually an English version of Caoimhín, which is the original name. It means 'handsome' and 'gentle'.

Latest record: Caoimhín ranked 231 with 19 newborns.
When records began: Kevin ranked 15 with 452 newborns.

Rua

Pronunciation: Rue-ah
Variations: Ruairí, Ruaidhrí, Ruadh, Ruadhán

Rua means 'red-haired' or 'red'. This name was well known over 800 years ago, as it was the name of the King of Connacht who was the last High King of Ireland.

Latest record: Rua ranked 302 with 13 newborns.
When records began: No record.

Cormac

Pronunciation: Cur-mac

Cormac mac Airt (son of Art) was one of the first High Kings of Ireland and the last name on this list. He's said to have lived during the time of the hero Fionn mac Cumhaill.

Latest record: Cormac ranked 139 with 37 newborns.
When records began: Cormac ranked 87 with 39 newborns.

STORIES BEHIND
Irish SURNAMES

Wait, what's up with those prefixes?

In Irish surnames, 'Mac' means 'son of' and 'O' means 'descendant of'. For daughters, it's 'Ni' and 'Nic'.

Murphy

Variations: Mac Murchadha, O'Murchu, Ó Murchadha

Murphy is the most common surname in Ireland, with about 55,000 people bearing the name. It means 'descendant of Murchadh', Murchadh being a sea-warrior. It's also the most common Irish surname in America, where there are 308,417 Murphys. That is one hell of a clan. It is more people than there are in most of the 32 counties of Ireland. Galway, the fifth largest county, only has a population of 277,737, after all.

O'Neill

Variations: O'Neal, Uí Néill

While the Murphys are clearly a charming bunch, a single individual, Niall of the Nine Hostages, might have been the most prolific male in Irish history. Recently geneticists at Trinity College Dublin found that 21% of men from north-western Ireland, and even 2% of men from New York, share his Y-chromosome haplotype. A biography of Niall can be constructed from several sources, including *The Book of the Taking of Ireland (Lebor Gabála Érenn)*, which is about a thousand years old.

O'Connor

Variations: Ó Conaire, Ó Conchubhair

The O'Connor clan claimed to be descendants of the Irish mythological figures, the Tuatha Dé Danann. The famous symbol of Ireland, the Irish harp, was the instrument of their chief god, The Dagda.

O'Brien

Variation: Ó Briain

Descendants of Brian Boru, the first king who could truly claim to rule the entire island of Ireland, known as the High King of Ireland. The O'Briens played a crucial role in Irish history, particularly during the Battle of Clontarf, which took place over 1,000 years ago. In this battle an estimated 10,000 men died, marking the end of Viking dominance in Ireland.

McCarthy

Variation: Mac Cartaigh

The McCarthys were the sworn enemies of the O'Briens. The name 'McCarthy' means 'son of Carthaigh', a name derived from the Old Irish word *cairptech*, meaning 'chariot driver'.

Kelly

Variations: Ó Ceallaigh, O'Kelly

The Kellys predate Jesus himself. They came from the tribe of Ui Maine, with origins from the third wave of Celts to settle in Ireland in the first century BC.

Sullivan

Variations: Ó Súilleabháin, O'Sullivan

This name is derived from the Irish word *súil*, meaning 'eye'. Some say the name means 'hawk-eyed' or 'dark-eyed', implying someone with a keen or fierce gaze; a cute hoor.

Murray

Variations: Muiredach (Old Irish), Muireadhach, Muireach, Murdoch

In old Irish Muiredach means master, and there's been a few around for a long time. Muiredach Bolgrach was the name given to a very early ruler of the entire island of Ireland. This High King of Ireland ruled some time between 893 BC and 674 BC depending on sources.

Doyle

Variation: Ó Dubhghaill

The surname Doyle is derived from the Irish Ó Dubhghaill, meaning 'descendant of the dark stranger', from the Irish words *dubh*, 'dark', and *gall*, 'stranger/foreigner'. The 'dark stranger' in question likely refers to the Norse-Gaelic settlers, descendants of the Vikings.

Brennan

Variation: Ó Braonáin

The surname Brennan derives from Ó Braonáin, meaning 'descendant of Braonán', a name associated with the word *braon*, meaning 'sorrow', 'tear' or 'drop'. Here's to the Brennans, descendants of sorrow, but sure give them a pint and they'll be smiling.

There is an Irish saying: *'Ní dhiúltódh sé braon beag'*, 'He wouldn't refuse a little drop.'

TOP 20 MOST COMMON IRISH FAMILY NAMES

Rank	Surname	Occurrences
1	Murphy	582
2	Kelly	443
3	Byrne	383
4	O'Brien	354
5	Walsh	354
6	Ryan	347
7	O'Connor	288
8	O'Sullivan	287
9	Doyle	244
10	McCarthy	242
11	O'Neill	225
12	O'Reilly	180
13	Lynch	177
14	Murray	177
15	Dunne	176
16	Burke	171
17	McDonagh	163
18	Daly	162
19	Kennedy	160
20	Ward	154

NAMES
by NUMBERS

*It's interesting to see how the popularity of Irish names
has changed over the past 60 years.
We hope this chapter gives you more inspiration.*

Time to pick your baby's name!

When we compare 2024 and 1964, we can see that in recent years there is a much greater variety of names for newborn girls in Ireland. Back in 1964 everyone was given the same names; Mary, Catherine and Margaret were extremely common. In a single year, the top three names were give to 6,000 babies. By comparison, in 2024, the top three names were given to a little under a thousand babies and that's despite the population doubling since then.

Comparing the lists of boys' names, names that have typically been thought of as Roman Catholic have dropped out of the top spots and been replaced by traditional Irish names. This is reflective of modern Irish society and the Vatican's dwindling influence.

Back in 1964, Irish parents weren't exactly known for their daring name choices. Over half of the boys born that year ended up with one of the top 10 names. Another notable aspect of the boys' name lists is the enduring popularity of James, Daniel, Michael and Thomas, which remain in the top 20 names in both lists. This is unlike the girls' lists, where none of the top 20 names being picked now were in the top 20 list back in the day.

TOP 10 BABY NAMES AS GAEILGE

GIRLS' NAMES

Rank	Name	Occurrences
2	Éabha	293
5	Fiadh	286
16	Croía	188
24	Saoirse	164
31	Caoimhe	131
33	Róisín	126
37	Cara	118
38	Sadhbh	117
40	Éala	114
42	Clodagh	109

BOYS' NAMES

Rank	Name	Occurrences
3	Rían	432
4	Cillian	352
6	Tadhg	318
7	Fionn	304
8	Liam	303
9	Oisín	286
15	Seán	222
16	Patrick	220
19	Conor	210
22	Páidí	201

TOP 100 BOYS' and GIRLS' NAMES IN IRELAND (2024)

GIRLS' NAMES

Rank	Name	Occurrences
1	Sophie	294
2	Éabha	293
3	Grace	291
4	Emily	290
5	Fiadh	286
6	Lily	253
7	Olivia	246
8	Amelia	220
9	Sadie	216
10	Mia	213
11	Lucy	204
12	Freya	196
13	Isla	193
14	Ella	192
15	Ellie	190
16	Croía	188
17	Emma	187
17	Maya	187
19	Sophia	180

Rank	Name	Occurrences
20	Chloe	179
20	Hannah	179
22	Molly	171
23	Evie	167
24	Saoirse	164
25	Sofia	154
26	Ava	152
27	Robyn	148
28	Millie	145
29	Anna	140
30	Ruby	134
31	Caoimhe	131
31	Rosie	131
33	Róisín	126
34	Bonnie	123
35	Erin	120
35	Isabelle	120
37	Cara	118
38	Sadhbh	117
39	Holly	115
40	Éala	114
41	Annie	112
42	Clodagh	109
42	Daisy	109
44	Hazel	108
45	Aoife	107
45	Katie	107
47	Kate	106
47	Willow	106

Rank	Name	Occurrences
49	Maisie	105
50	Ada	104
50	Méabh	104
52	Alice	103
53	Leah	102
54	Ayla	100
55	Isabella	99
56	Fíadh	93
56	Sienna	93
58	Eva	91
59	Zoe	89
60	Ivy	88
61	Aria	87
61	Sarah	87
63	Harper	86
64	Charlotte	84
65	Ailbhe	83
65	Clara	83
65	Zara	83
68	Faye	82
69	Layla	79
70	Rose	77
71	Maeve	76
72	Mila	74
73	Elsie	72
73	Maria	72
75	Aoibhín	67
75	Julia	67
77	Cora	66

Rank	Name	Occurrences
78	Lottie	65
79	Abigail	64
79	Eve	64
81	Elizabeth	63
82	Emilia	62
82	Phoebe	62
84	Nora	61
85	Evelyn	59
85	Hallie	59
87	Georgia	58
87	Heidi	58
89	Hailey	54
89	Poppy	54
91	Ciara	53
91	Mollie	53
93	Rhea	52
94	Isabel	51
94	Niamh	51
96	Luna	49
96	Nina	49
98	Aurora	48
98	Bella	48
98	Caragh	48
98	Laoise	48
98	Síofra	48
103	Ayda	47
103	Stella	47

BOYS' NAMES

Rank	Name	Occurrences
1	Jack	490
2	Noah	486
3	Rían	432
4	Cillian	352
5	James	336
6	Tadhg	318
7	Fionn	304
8	Liam	303
9	Oisín	286
10	Charlie	258
11	Daniel	257
12	Finn	255
13	Theo	252
14	Thomas	226
15	Seán	222
16	Patrick	220
17	Michael	218
18	Luke	217
19	Conor	210
20	Harry	209
21	Tommy	202
22	Leo	201
22	Páidí	201
24	Luca	197
25	Adam	188
26	Darragh	184
27	Oliver	181

Rank	Name	Occurrences
28	Bobby	179
29	John	168
30	Jamie	162
30	Kai	162
32	Oscar	159
33	Cian	158
33	Max	158
35	Ollie	157
36	Alex	155
37	Callum	154
38	Sonny	147
39	Dylan	141
40	David	134
41	Ben	132
42	Matthew	131
43	Caelan	128
44	Alexander	127
45	Muhammad	126
46	Ryan	124
47	Arthur	119
48	Arlo	118
49	Alfie	117
50	Shay	107
51	Archie	105
51	Ethan	105
51	Freddie	105
51	Sam	105
55	Tom	103
56	Billy	102

Rank	Name	Occurrences
56	Mason	102
56	Theodore	102
59	Senan	99
60	Hugo	93
60	Leon	93
62	Jake	92
63	Evan	90
64	Jacob	89
65	Donnacha	88
65	Ronan	88
67	William	87
68	Rory	86
68	Teddy	86
70	Joseph	83
70	Nathan	83
70	Samuel	83
73	Joshua	80
74	Benjamin	79
74	Danny	79
74	Frankie	79
74	Lucas	79
78	Joey	78
79	Aaron	77
80	Daithí	76
81	Odhrán	73
81	Tomás	73
83	Jude	71
84	Aidan	70
85	Louis	68

Rank	Name	Occurrences
86	Logan	66
87	Odhran	65
88	Cathal	63
88	Cody	63
88	George	63
91	Caleb	61
91	Rowan	61
91	Ted	61
94	Dáithí	60
94	Jayden	60
94	Mark	60
97	Robert	58
98	Ruairí	57
99	Henry	56
99	Iarlaith	56
99	Isaac	56
102	Anthony	55
102	Dáire	55
102	Paddy	55

TOP 100 BOYS' and GIRLS' NAMES IN IRELAND (1964)

GIRLS' NAMES

Rank	Name	Occurrences
1	Mary	3471
2	Catherine	1412
3	Margaret	1392
4	Ann	866
5	Anne	834
6	Elizabeth	722
7	Caroline	617
8	Bridget	595
9	Geraldine	579
10	Patricia	536
11	Jacqueline	529
12	Pauline	460
13	Helen	437
14	Deirdre	408
15	Bernadette	392
16	Sandra	358
17	Eileen	344

Rank	Name	Occurrences
18	Martina	339
19	Teresa	328
20	Paula	311
21	Carmel	304
22	Susan	303
23	Kathleen	301
24	Angela	291
25	Josephine	287
26	Marie	284
27	Ellen	282
28	Linda	279
29	Brigid	272
30	Nora	264
31	Joan	262
32	Fiona	249
33	Maria	236
34	Anna	214
35	Siobhan	207
36	Carol	185
37	Sheila	176
38	Frances	173
39	Sharon	172
40	Christina	169
41	Karen	165
42	Julia	157
43	Barbara	156
44	Johanna	146
45	Yvonne	139
46	Sarah	137

Rank	Name	Occurrences
47	Lorraine	135
47	Colette	135
49	Rose	130
50	Valerie	129
51	Veronica	126
52	Orla	120
53	Miriam	117
54	Louise	116
55	Clare	115
56	Denise	113
57	Alice	111
58	Elaine	107
59	Jane	106
59	Rita	106
61	Theresa	100
62	Grainne	99
63	Helena	98
63	Brenda	98
65	Christine	92
65	Noreen	92
67	Suzanne	91
68	Jennifer	90
68	Annette	90
70	Monica	87
71	Rosemary	86
72	Philomena	84
72	Olive	84
74	Adrienne	80
75	Claire	78

Rank	Name	Occurrences
76	Deborah	77
77	Katherine	76
78	Jean	75
78	Marian	75
80	Maeve	74
80	Dolores	74
80	Rosaleen	74
83	Edel	73
83	Evelyn	73
85	Irene	72
85	Audrey	72
87	Ruth	70
87	Una	70
87	Imelda	70
90	Nuala	68
91	Hannah	67
91	Maureen	67
93	Jacinta	66
93	Winifred	66
95	Dorothy	65
95	Antoinette	65
95	Majella	65
98	Eleanor	64
98	Ursula	64
100	Aileen	63

BOYS' NAMES

Rank	Name	Occurrences
1	John	3696
2	Patrick	2235
3	Michael	2157
4	Paul	1814
5	James	1554
6	Thomas	1349
7	David	936
8	William	875
9	Martin	849
10	Gerard	815
11	Joseph	737
12	Anthony	613
13	Peter	527
14	Brian	464
15	Kevin	452
16	Francis	429
17	Brendan	426
18	Edward	425
19	Daniel	395
20	Noel	394
21	Denis	347
22	Robert	342
23	Declan	321
24	Richard	301
25	Stephen	296
26	Timothy	295
27	Christopher	289

Rank	Name	Occurrences
28	Mark	279
29	Alan	245
30	Raymond	237
30	Derek	237
32	Kieran	224
33	Bernard	201
34	Andrew	195
34	Dermot	195
36	Philip	187
37	Aidan	182
38	Sean	171
39	Jeremiah	161
39	Cornelius	161
41	Kenneth	150
42	Vincent	148
43	Charles	145
43	Desmond	145
45	Colm	144
45	Donal	144
47	Niall	142
48	Laurence	141
49	Ciaran	124
50	Eugene	123
51	Maurice	120
52	George	115
53	Hugh	112
54	Liam	111
55	Terence	102
56	Conor	97

Rank	Name	Occurrences
57	Gerald	94
58	Nicholas	92
59	Matthew	89
60	Seamus	87
60	Henry	87
62	Ian	86
62	Eamon	86
64	Eamonn	83
65	Adrian	75
66	Fergus	71
67	Ronan	70
68	Oliver	69
69	Barry	62
70	Finbarr	61
71	Owen	59
72	Gabriel	57
73	Rory	56
73	Damian	56
75	Shane	49
75	Damien	49
75	Enda	49
78	Gregory	47
78	Garrett	47
80	Edmond	45
81	Bartholomew	44
82	Neil	43
83	Eoin	42
84	Gary	41
84	Dominic	41

Rank	Name	Occurrences
86	Karl	40
87	Cormac	39
88	Padraig	38
89	Colin	37
89	Ronald	37
91	Simon	36
91	Leslie	36
93	Fergal	35
94	Eric	34
94	Aiden	34
96	Cathal	32
96	Keith	32
98	Arthur	31
98	Nigel	31
100	Fintan	29

Hopefully one day the ancient Irish names in this book will be resurrected and reclaim their rightful places as the most popular names in Ireland. Look out, Jack. Balor the cyclops has his eye on the top spot. These names also just sound fantastic, now that you're pronouncing them right.